MW00477374

THE CANAANITE WOMAN

THE CANAANITE WOMAN

Poems

Aug. 22. 22
Alexandria, VA

Benjamin Bagocius

For Betsy
Your belief in me and my work
has meant more than you can know.

Thank you for the deep-and-wide
work you do of loving, speaking,
listening, noticing, feeling, creat-
ing, and crafting belonging. I
treasure the insights you share
out in any gathering, as well as

RESOURCE *Publications* · Eugene, Oregon

the quiet power of your listening
and present attention. Your words
and presence are both grounding
and elevating.   ♡ ☀ Ben

THE CANAANITE WOMAN
Poems

Copyright © 2022 Benjamin Bagocius. All rights reserved. Except for brief quotations in critical publications or reviews, no part of this book may be reproduced in any manner without prior written permission from the publisher. Write: Permissions, Wipf and Stock Publishers, 199 W. 8th Ave., Suite 3, Eugene, OR 97401.

Resource Publications
An Imprint of Wipf and Stock Publishers
199 W. 8th Ave., Suite 3
Eugene, OR 97401

www.wipfandstock.com

PAPERBACK ISBN: 978-1-6667-3251-1
HARDCOVER ISBN: 978-1-6667-2631-2
EBOOK ISBN: 978-1-6667-2632-9

VERSION NUMBER 061422

Scripture quotations marked (NIV) are taken from the Holy Bible, New International Version®, NIV®. Copyright © 1973, 1978, 1984, 2011 by Biblica, Inc.™ Used by permission of Zondervan. All rights reserved worldwide. www.zondervan.com. The "NIV" and "New International Version" are trademarks registered in the United States Patent and Trademark Office by Biblica, Inc.™

The book is based on real events, though it also draws from literary, biblical, apocryphal, and imagined details. Thus, events and characters in the book are composites of this broad range of source material, details from which have been rearranged, reconceptualized, reimagined, and sometimes amplified for the sake of the story. All characters, events, and points of view in the narrative are meant to tell a poetic story and neither speak for nor represent anyone or anything outside the narrative.

For all Canaanite Women and Men
across time,
and for my parents, Paul and Cindy

A Canaanite woman from that vicinity came to him, crying out,
"Lord, Son of David, have mercy on me!
My daughter is demon-possessed and suffering terribly."

—MATTHEW 15:22 (NIV)

There is amongst us one Justa, a Syro-Phœnician, by race a Canaanite,
whose daughter was oppressed with a grievous disease.
And she came to our Lord, crying out, and entreating
that He would heal her daughter.

—THE CLEMENTINE HOMILIES, CHAPTER XIX

CONTENTS

Acknowledgements | xi

Nevertheless, She Persisted:
  A Tribute to the Canaanite Woman | xiii

The Canaanite Woman and her Daughter Refine Jesus's Taste | 1

The Canaanite Woman Helps Jesus Climb Higher Up
  the Mountain | 3

The Canaanite Woman Heals Jesus | 5

Daily Walk | 8

The Canaanite Woman's Bookshelf | 10

Street Market | 11

Curling Iron | 13

The Canaanite Woman as a Girl | 14

Street Vendors Do Not Know the Canaanite Woman Has Saved
  Their Wares from Destruction | 15

Clement, the Dog | 16

Bernice Walks Clement | 17

Bernice Shares Why She Pulls the Wagon | 18

The Bazaar | 19

Bernice Cannot Understand the World's Madness | 21

Shach Sets Up His Board for the Illat Kalbeμ Tournament | 22

The Canaanite Woman Gets One Breath | 23

Bernice Will Never Understand the World's Madness | 25

Bernice Makes Sure I Know It's Dinnertime | 26

Bernice Loves, or The Aunt Checks Instagram | 27

The Family and I Walk out of the Mall | 28

The Aunt Has a Moment of Understanding God | 29

Bernice Always Walks Beside Her Mom. She Won't Walk
    with Anyone Else | 30

The Family Takes a Trip to the Lighthouse | 31

Uncle Esh Makes a Surprise Visit | 32

The Family Never Made it to the Lighthouse | 33

We all Resurrect | 36

Disability Services I | 37

Disability Services II | 38

Writing with Bernice | 41

The Aunt Receives a Thank You Card in the Mail | 43

The Aunt Remembers the Outdoor Concert | 44

The Aunt Hears Bernice's Laughter | 45

The Tutor Logs a Missed Appointment | 46

Odd Lean | 48

Daisies in a Jar | 50

Bernice Fishing | 52

Shach Doesn't Want Anything for His Birthday | 54

Bernice Triumphs in the Kitchen | 55

The Canaanite Woman Sees Bernice Triumph
    in the Kitchen | 56

Bernice's Aunt Has a Demon | 57

The Family Leaves the Beach a Day Early | 58

The Canaanite Woman Sees a Rainbow | 59

The Canaanite Young Woman Goes to College | 60

The Canaanite Woman's Seventh Book | 61

Mom, Mom | 62

Matthew and Mark Only Got Part of It | 64

The Aunt's Arrival | 65

The Canaanite Woman Catches Her Breath | 68

The Living Room is Dark, Empty, and Quiet | 70

The Hospital Policemen | 71

The Canaanite Woman Does Mountain Pose | 73

Queen Mother | 74

Bernice Visits Her Grandparents | 75

Rainbow Talk Time | 76

Shach's Rainbow Talk Time | 77

Bernice Goes to Bed | 78

The Canaanite Woman Looks Out the Kitchen Window
at Night. She Sees Herself Illuminating | 79

The Canaanite Woman Sits Atop the Boulder | 80

Jesus's Chief of Staff Emails the Canaanite Woman | 83

The Canaanite Woman Reads the Email | 85

Notes | 87

ACKNOWLEDGEMENTS

I wish to thank the editors of the following journals for publishing earlier versions of this book's poems, and sometimes under different titles:

Dark Moon Lilith: "The Canaanite Woman Heals Jesus"

Rat's Ass Review: "Writing with Bernice," "The Auntie Receives a Thank You Card in the Mail," "Bernice Triumphs in the Kitchen," "The Canaanite Woman Sees Bernice Triumph in the Kitchen," "The Canaanite Woman Reads the Email."

My deepest gratitude also goes to the following people for their support and encouragement during the writing of this book:

My parents, Paul and Cindy Bagocius; my siblings Deborah Bagocius, Scott Bagocius, and Diana Dunn; my grandfather G. Douglas Hudson; friends and fellow writers, artists, and teachers Katherine Judith Anderson, Blayne Barnes, Deborah Ann Krishnan, Mary Anne Burrows, Megan Coder, David Conrad, Jennifer Eccher, Rebecca Kent, Carol Kandiko, Tanja Kummerfeld, Betsy Nero, Helene Pasquin, Aryakorn Joy Phaphouvaninh, Angelina Rodríguez, Tera Stubblefield, and Christine Ticknor.

NEVERTHELESS, SHE PERSISTED

A Tribute to the Canaanite Woman

The figure of the Canaanite Woman has commanded respect and admiration from writers since antiquity. Despite this high regard, surprisingly little has been written or imagined about her life beyond her encounter with Jesus of Nazareth in the Gospels. The Canaanite Woman appears in both the Books of Matthew and Mark, writers who narrate her asking Jesus to heal her daughter's suffering from so-called demon possession (see Matthew 15:22 and Mark 7:26). Modern-day readers tend to push back on the expression "demon possession" for its vilifying of those with complicated behaviors or rare disorders. But what also stands out to me about this term is that the Gospel writers, not the Canaanite Woman, write the language of demon possession to describe the girl's behavior. We cannot assume that the Canaanite Woman herself uses this term to describe her daughter or her daughter's experience, because we do not have the Canaanite Woman's account of the story. The Canaanite Woman, as the girl's mother, likely understood the complexity of her daughter's behaviors in a much more nuanced and full-dimensional fashion than Matthew's and Mark's expression suggests. After all, the Gospel writers are episodic onlookers rather than fulltime participants in the Canaanite Woman's and her daughter's lives. Thus both Matthew and Mark perhaps come to a hasty, limited, and oversimplified conclusion about both daughter and mother.

The Gospel writers narrate Jesus, too, coming to an impulsive conclusion about the Canaanite Woman and her daughter.

In Matthew's and Mark's accounts, Jesus dismisses the Canaanite Woman and her plea for support, comparing her to a dog who should not expect to receive scraps from the master's table (see Matthew 15:26 and Mark 7:27). Yet in both Gospels, the Canaanite Woman persists despite this insult. She is intent on creating a life of thriving for her daughter and herself in a culture that marginalizes living with experiences we might understand today as complicated behaviors or disorders. In Gospel versions, the Canaanite Woman continues to state her case, correcting Jesus's limited idea of love and persuading him to expand his definition of it. Yet Matthew and Mark give the Canaanite Woman's story only a handful of verses before moving on to Jesus's next encounter. For Matthew and Mark, the Canaanite Woman is a supporting actor, since their protagonist is Jesus of Nazareth.

The present book does not adopt Matthew's and Mark's language of demon possession to describe the girl's complexity. However, the book does draw out Matthew's and Mark's details of the Canaanite Woman's distress and her determination to alleviate her daughter's suffering associated with a complex condition that the community tries little to understand. The book unfolds Gospel writers' narrations of pain and fortitude, desperation and persistence expressed by the Canaanite Woman in a culture that casts aside both her daughter's experience and her own as a parent of a child with complicated behaviors.

I wrote the book to honor the experiences of mothers of children with complex behaviors and rare disorders. The Canaanite Woman, to me, is a visionary, and as such, a leader. She perceives a vulnerable person's full dimensionality in a community that cannot or will not see it, and she insists that those in positions of power evolve their imaginations about what it means to love. The purpose of the book is to follow the Canaanite Woman's lead in expanding a community's limited imagination and constricting ideologies of so-called ability and disability; to affirm reverence for the nearly limitless variety of developmental, physical, and psychological differences among the human family; to extend calls for greater compassion, understanding, and equity for all members of that human family; to support parents, families, and caregivers of people with complicated behaviors and rare disorders who persist and thrive in spite of countless everyday social, political, and material obstacles; and to widen education, research, and hearts to human diversity so that parents of children with challenging behaviors receive supports to ensure their thriving in a culture of radical belonging.

To be sure, what counts as a disorder is often less a biological given than it is a set of ideological assumptions. Traits deemed so-called disordered, disabled, or dysfunctional often point to room where a community's imagination and built environment could expand beyond its small parameters. After all, traits that one community might understand as falling under disorder or impairment could be considered normal, sacred, or a non-issue in another community, depending on conventions engrained in education, sports, economics, governance, and religion, as well as embedded within assumptions about gender, age, race, ethnicity, class, public and private space, family, and nation, for instance. Any number of difficulties faced by individuals, families, and advocates in the challenging-behavior community might, arguably, lie less in a so-called disorder and more in a wider culture's underdeveloped imagination of what ability looks, sounds, and acts like. I write these things neither to deny the very real experiences of individuals and families in the complex behaviors and rare disorders communities, nor to disavow the challenges and assets that accompany these journeys. Yet even as we use terms such as complex behaviors, disorder, or disability to revere diversity, extend dignity, and widen equity across our shared public life together, I believe givens about what constitutes disorder or disability should always be reexamined. Becoming too satisfied with received ideas about order and disorder, ability and disability narrows the potential of everyone. When we expand our imagination, creativity, and even play on these topics, then everyone's lives in the community expands as well.

In Gospel narratives, the Canaanite Woman launches this imaginative expansion. Unfolding her story further, I join other writers who honor the Canaanite Woman's subtle yet fierce leadership. About two hundred years after Matthew's and Mark's narratives, around 200 to 300 AD, a writer who has come to be called Clement would take up the story of the Canaanite Woman. In *The Clementine Homilies*, Clement—reputably a former companion of the apostle Peter, one of Jesus's leading disciples—records Peter's teachings and discourse. According to Clement, Peter identifies the Canaanite Woman as one Justa and her daughter as Bernice. By giving mother and daughter proper names, Clement's writing humanizes the two female figures more than do Matthew's and Mark's accounts. Clement refers to the girl's experience not as demon-possession but as a "grievous disease."[1] Acknowledging aspects of "grievous" pain associated with Bernice's experience, Clement nonetheless refuses to vilify the girl or her journey. By moving away from Gospel writers' language of demon possession, Clement dignifies Justa as a woman fully aware of her daughter's multidimensional rather than flat personhood. *The Clementine Homilies* thus give mother and daughter more developed—that is to say, more human—narratives than Matthew's and Mark's accounts do.

Clement so reveres the Canaanite Woman that he explores her journey beyond her famous encounter with Jesus. In Clement's version, Justa and her husband divorce over her decision to follow the controversial teachings of Jesus, and Justa raises her daughter independently. Justa later rescues two boys from pirates by purchasing them. She adopts the boys as her sons and raises them to become prominent scholars and leaders in this new spiritual community. Clement's narrative thus adds more layers to Gospel accounts of the Canaanite Woman. Though *The Clementine Homilies*, like Matthew's and Mark's versions, describe the Canaanite Woman as an independent thinker and determined advocate for vulnerable community members, Clement's text primarily records the experiences and journeys of men such as the reputed author, Peter, and Simon Magus. Justa functions, as in the Gospels, as a

---

1. Clement, *The Clementine Homilies*, translated by Thomas Smith, James Donaldson, and Peter Peterson (Edinburgh: T. & T. Clark, 1870), 40.

minor character. By leaving so much left unsaid about her, Clement's text—like the Gospels—invites other writers to elaborate, imagine, and tell more of the Canaanite Woman's story.

I learned from Matthew, Mark, Clement, and other spiritual writers to write narrative verse about an inspiring leader worthy of awe. My version of the Canaanite Woman does not align exactly with Clement's version, just as his narrative does not exactly follow Matthew's, and just as Matthew's account does not exactly overlap with Mark's. My book shines a more sustained and therefore different quality of light on the Canaanite Woman, who emerges as a prophet when we pause to notice both her inborn and hard-won wisdom, her strength and resilience as a mother of a child with complex behaviors in a culture that tends to look away when she asks for support, understanding, and community.

Nevertheless, she persists.

The Canaanite Woman, to me, is not a bygone visionary from an outdated story. She lives here and now. She is your server at the restaurant. Your business partner. Your sister. Your mother. Your wife. Your friend. She is the woman seated beside you on the bleachers at the soccer game. Your yoga teacher. The woman driving the car in the next lane. She might be a man, for men, too, are often primary caretakers of children with complicated behaviors. Maybe you are the Canaanite Woman. Or will be.

So invisible has this woman's experience been to our eyes, so untrained are our ears to hear her sustained message, that her wisdom often sounds strange—even illegible—to our unseasoned ears. Many of this book's scenes, in both their pain and joys, may seem so unimaginable they could not possibly reflect the Canaanite Woman's everyday lived experiences. Even Jesus does not know what to make of the Canaanite Woman's story in the Gospels. Yet as one poem states about the Canaanite Woman's resurrection, her decision to rise again after devastation and step once more into the unkempt but fragrant garden of life: "Let others be shocked."

The Canaanite Woman invites us to shift our gaze from Jesus's stardom to a quieter light: the Canaanite Woman's. I wrote this book to listen to and learn what the Canaanite Woman has to teach us about the Mystery of Love and its nearly unnoticeable power to dissolve rigid ideas about self, other, and our lives together. Let's follow her. The Canaanite Woman will lead us to other quiet visionaries along the way, including ones we often pass by: the visionary within the marginalized, the visionary within oneself.

For more information and to support research, advocacy, and families in the complicated behaviors and rare disorders communities, please visit the National Institute of Health's Genetic and Rare Diseases Information Center (rarediseases.info.nih.gov), Children's National Rare Disease Institute (childrensnational.org/ departments/rare-disease-institute), the National Organization for Rare Disorders (rarediseases.org), Parents and Researchers Interested in Smith-Magenis Syndrome (PRISMS) (prisms.org), as well as your local community, resource, and outreach centers that advocate for the health and wellness of children, adults, and families in all their sacred diversity.

THE CANAANITE WOMAN AND HER
DAUGHTER REFINE JESUS'S TASTE

I left home with my daughter Bernice before dawn
to see Jesus, visiting three towns over.
Bernice could attack me
or run at any moment,
so I brought snacks, video games,
and her phone to occupy her.

I'm quiet, so I asked Ba'alat
to give me the voice to ask Jesus
in front of everyone
in the temple courtyard
to heal my child from her suffering.

Bernice ripped apart books and smashed windows.

My brother could no longer restrain her
when she flipped over tables at market
or went after her little sister.

Schools would not admit her.
I was running out of places to hide the knives.
I feared sleep. Another morning getting closer.

Jesus paused at my request,
then compared me to a dog

lucky to get any fresh bread
the master may happen to throw it.

I took a breath.

Perhaps, I replied, but each dog
has their own hungers. Clement—our dog—
won't eat wheat, only rye.

And only after we remove the crust,
Bernice added.

THE CANAANITE WOMAN HELPS JESUS CLIMB
HIGHER UP THE MOUNTAIN

Jesus left there and . . . went up a mountainside and sat down. Great
crowds came to him, bringing the lame, the blind, the crippled, the
mute and many others. . . . After Jesus had sent the crowd away, he got
into the boat and went to the vicinity of Magadan.
—MATTHEW 15:29–30, 39 (NIV)

As if he had climbed higher up a mountain,
Jesus had reached a higher consciousness.
He now saw the foreigner, the lame, blind, crippled, mute, and
     many others
as God, God, God, God, God, and God

whom he could leave and did.
He had to be in Magadan before nightfall.

Washing his face
before retiring to bed
in a small Magadan house,
Jesus thought of the Canaanite Woman
who made a home
atop crevasses, crags,
and falling rock
with God who needed

to learn how to brush Her teeth
and write Her name
and sit for five hours in a bumpy cart
under a burning sun
down the mountain to Tyre
to see a promising but
amateur climber named Jesus.

If the Canaanite Woman ever went to Magadan,
this God came with her.

How do you convince God She needs
to sit for five hours in a rickety cart
or learn to hold a pencil,
Jesus wondered as he drifted off to sleep,
not needing to come up with an answer
to these questions.

THE CANAANITE WOMAN HEALS JESUS

The story is that I, Jesus, healed her child.
But I didn't. The Canaanite woman healed me.

She showed me how far away from God I was.
I thought I lived in God's palace. But I hadn't
yet even reached His front door.

I would only touch the afflicted, then leave.
I wouldn't live with them.
I didn't make them breakfast.
I didn't place pencils back into their hands,
teaching them to write after they stabbed me with them.
I didn't clean up shattered glass
of the framed paintings I had devoted months to making,
which took only one second for the afflicted to knock
to the floor and slash with a knife.
I didn't cook them dinner an hour later
and walk the dog with them as the sun set.
I never leapt from the car into interstate traffic
after the afflicted who had bolted from the passenger seat
into oncoming semis. I didn't sit overnight
in the hospital with the afflicted after
they yelled "Fuck you!" to me while tearing the seven books
I had written before they raced down the street
to send jars of pickles, applesauce, and wine
smashing to the ground at market

again. I didn't meet with endless series of doctors
through endless emergency-room nights, then drive to different
pharmacies for the afflicted's medication while they slept.
I never secured the afflicted's seat belt, drove them home,
and tucked them into bed.
I never signed them up for swimming lessons.

I asked the Canaanite Woman to join my ministry
and preach with me, because she was an expert in
The Mystery, the expanse
beyond the brick
limits of love.

She said no.

She had to raise her two daughters and son,
rewrite her books,
and write new ones.

DAILY WALK

"Mom. Mom."

Each crunch of gravel
comes with "Mom." *Crunch.* "Mom." *Crunch.*

Bernice needs her mom, Justa,
to remind her they're getting
candied figs after the hike.

I'm Bernice's aunt, Justa's sister.
We're pausing together near a boulder.

"Mom. Mom."
"Yes, figs," Justa answers.
"After we're done hiking, Mom. Mom."
"Look at your schedule," which Justa has drawn on parchment.
Some days Bernice destroys it. Most times she loses it.

It's often best not to give Bernice a schedule.
When there's change she melts down. Think of
a cart barreling through fog,
road obscured from sidewalk.
A crowded street market lies ahead.
Tables full of smashable plates.
No table bolted to the ground.

Justa calibrates her speed to Bernice's
and scans the horizon for blindspots.
Rests are breaths.

"Mom. Mom."
"Yes, after hiking."

Eshta, her younger daughter, has run ahead and found a rock.
She races back to show us.
It sparkles everywhere you turn it.

"Mom. Mom!"
"Yes, Bernice. Figs. Beautiful, Eshta."
"Figs, then fishing, right Mom? Mom!"
"What does the schedule show?"
"I don't have it. Mom! Mom!"
"Yes, fishing."
"Then what, Mom?" *Crunch.* "Mom." *Crunch.*

THE CANAANITE WOMAN'S BOOKSHELF

We writers rest on bookshelves.
Etty Hillesum. Jalāl ad-Dīn Muhammad Rūmī.
Emily Dickinson. Once we are dead, our new work begins.
We move into the innermost castle of readers,
hauling our goods into their lives,
our sentences our carts.
We sit in the heart's stone rooms lit by candlelight.
We do not interrupt dinners. When the daughter takes a chair
and smashes it into the living room window,
sunlight streams in.
No more filtering the light. And by nightfall
the dark.

STREET MARKET

At the street market, Bernice enjoys sugared figs.
Scents of jasmine and curry waft from vendors.
Tea for sale, sweetened with honey.
Justa has run out of coins.

Mom, mom. Can I get a sweet tea? Mom. Mom.

Justa hears Bernice's jaw tighten,
smells smoke from the basement
of her daughter's eyes.

Maybe later, Bernice, Justa replies,
making sure the nearest exit
is still where she saw it when they entered.
It seems to inch further away.

Her son Shach grieves, *Bernice is shutting down again.*
Handmade jewelry and bowls cover tables.
Justa sees the temple bazaar
Bernice destroyed two months ago. Necklaces
tangled across the rubble, ceramic shards littered
the ground like bullet casings. Red wine dripped
from tablecloths like a massacre.
The smashed plates inside her.

Justa has seconds
to coax the reigns from Bernice's rage
and guide those horses delicately, delicately
away from handmade bracelets and bowls, away
from tents whose posts are thin as toothpicks.

Think of sticking your arms through shattered glass
to save sleeping vendors and shoppers
from a fire they do not know has started.

CURLING IRON

I learned beauty was deliberate by watching Justa make it.
A teenager, she arranged the coals, heated the iron.
Took a tuft of bang, rolled it around the iron,
held it for eight, nine, ten seconds.
Then moved to the next tuft.

I was scared of the iron.
Holding fire like a sword? I wouldn't touch it.

She held the quiet flame
centimeters from her skin,
coaxed straightness to bend,
each curl a feat of muscular patience.

Her shoulders must've tired.
Eight, nine, ten.
Eight, nine, ten.

Eight, nine, ten.

THE CANAANITE WOMAN AS A GIRL

None of us get all of her *I*,
the letter moonlight writes across the sea,
fathoms deep.

STREET VENDORS DO NOT KNOW
THE CANAANITE WOMAN HAS SAVED
THEIR WARES FROM DESTRUCTION

At home Justa sweeps shards of shattered bowls,
emblazoned with her three children's names
in pieces across the floor.

"It could've been worse," she tells me. "All those vendors."
Bernice had wanted to go fishing. They hadn't brought her pole.
She had already been denied her figs. Her cells have a paper gate
to hold the storm.

Justa's son Shach moves the kitchen table so she can sweep
    underneath.
She tapes what glass remains in the window frame.

Shach steps in socks with the dustpan.
No afternoon run for Justa again.
She hopes to run tomorrow
before Shach's soccer practice.

She's making a book for the team,
assembling her photographs of their drills and goals.
She snapshots contemplation
on each boy's face
as they sit in the grass,
their turn to run, assist, and defend
coming up or right now.

CLEMENT, THE DOG

When the current tangles in the kitchen
I walk to Bernice and sit down.
I have an easy time with death
because I know it does not exist.
When Bernice knocks over the table,
forks and knives rain like spears.
My ears go down.
I know to make peace
less threatening.

My paws still
like all cores.

At these times Bernice does not register
my presence.
I am God.
Unimposing, the silent life
that waits, not for anything.
I was not taught who I am.

BERNICE WALKS CLEMENT

I walk him every day,
sometimes four or five times.
He's easier than
math. His paws don't write
story problems. He doesn't quite
believe in division. He's not a word
I have to sound out, his nose
and tail pronounce each silent vowel.
He always gives me the answer:
I'm glad you're here.
Let's be together.

BERNICE SHARES WHY SHE PULLS THE WAGON

Priestess Ana is sick, so no school today.
I get the wagon from the shed, and Shach
sits in it. I pull him down the street, trying to avoid
the bumps past the coffee vendor
to Mr. Yosef who sells oranges and blueberries,
tells us jokes and gives us honeyed dates from Athens,
bigger and sweeter than ones from Canaan.
Shach would never ask for them
so he's glad to have me to. He sits in the wagon
and nibbles like a rabbit. I eat mine in one gulp
then pull him home. Eshta's waiting for her turn.
Which is good because I wanted more dates
as big as Mr. Yosef's laugh.

THE BAZAAR

At the temple bazaar I enjoy almonds glazed with cinnamon,
watch children race past teenagers flirting and men smoking.
I notice Justa kneeling,
lacing Bernice's sandals. The light tightening
around my niece's eyes sounds *systems fail.*
I mouth to Justa, *Can I help?*

No, she replies.

Bernice has run out of tokens.
Her foot shakes like a rattle
snake. Sleepers hearing bump in the night,
a couple nearby lift their heads.
Justa has seconds.

She won't think about the expletives Bernice will hurl
at strangers as Justa brings her daughter to the cart, Bernice's
    shoulders
snaking from under Justa's grasp, the lunge she makes
to catch her daughter's arm, Justa won't think about the rock
    Bernice will grab
with her other hand, which Justa pries from her fingers before the
    girl hurls
it at onlookers, lucky enough to only have to watch, shame burn-
    ing Justa's face

as they watch her secure Bernice's thrashing body to her seat
    while the girl rips off the door handle
and throws it, hitting Justa's cheek now bleeding onto her new
    blouse,
Justa won't think about the boxes of peaches Bernice will smash,
    smearing sweet meat
across the seats, her blouse, the floor, her books, the holes Bernice
    will kick
inside her.

No, no, Justa won't think about that.
She's learned not to think about the future.
It's the only place she can go.

BERNICE CANNOT UNDERSTAND
THE WORLD'S MADNESS

A ribbon
of golden tokens
drops into my fingers
and leads me to a magical box
filled with bubbles
and balls which pour
like laughter
into my hands
Then suddenly the tokens
disappear and the stream
of colors stops
My forehead and eyes
get hot. The carnival
box crosses its arms
then shuts its glass face
to my open palms

SHACH SETS UP HIS BOARD
FOR THE ILLAT KALBEμ TOURNAMENT

I bring my clay board, unfold it, and lay it on the table.
I shake hands with my opponent, who's taller than me.
But from my height
I see more.
I'm always five steps ahead. I survey the entire board,
scan exits, imagine entries.
So many secrets and slidings
across rows and columns
on my kingdom
that I can fold up and carry with me
or put on a shelf.

THE CANAANITE WOMAN GETS ONE BREATH

"Mom. Mom!"

Bernice can't find the dog's leash
while Justa is on the phone
with billing from the psychiatric hospital
to which Bernice was admitted
for a few days after destroying the corner
market the first time.

"Here it is," Justa says, holding the leash to Bernice.

Bernice hasn't mastered the click onto the dog's collar.
Justa bends down to help her while giving
the account number to the representative.

Put on hold, Justa practices breathing. *Five more breaths,*
You can last five more breaths.

"Mom, the leash is stuck! Mom!"
Bernice's jaw stiffens. Justa hears the rattle.

Justa gets one breath to unravel the dog's leash.
The representative asks, "Hello? Hello?"

Bernice's rattle quickens. The door handle she could
grab and open.

Justa sees aisles of shattered glass lying like shrapnel, wine
gushing red across cereal boxes and smearing
across the floor where canned soups roll.

"Yes, yes, I'm here."

Justa is everywhere instantly

—market, hospital, bazaar—

like God.

BERNICE WILL NEVER UNDERSTAND THE WORLD'S MADNESS

Why can't the glass carnival
box overflow with colors like my heart?
I have rainbows bursting
inside me, the laughter I share
with Auntie when she inserts
her crumpled tokens,
her bad jokes, into the living room.
No one else laughs, but I do
because my glee comes in
teal and mauve and indigo rolling
roundness, which I offer to Auntie's
wide-open ears holding out their empty palms.

BERNICE MAKES SURE I KNOW IT'S DINNERTIME

I sit in my bedroom at my desk
lost in bureaucracy of licensing exams,
left behind life under waves of work emails.

Dinnertime, I hear my sister call out from the kitchen
below. Her call sounds like a ship about to sail, a vessel
too far for me to board in time.
Another missed trip.

On board, Bernice's brother Shach finds one more treasure
in his video game. Her sister Eshta gives
a treat to their pet rabbit. Bernice races upstairs,

knocks on my door.
Auntie, Auntie,
It's dinnertime.

She waits for me
from behind the door
to confirm *Ok thank you.*

She is not leaving without me.
She has jumped off the ship to get me.

BERNICE LOVES, OR THE AUNT CHECKS INSTAGRAM

Dear Friends, let us love one another, for love comes from God. Everyone who loves has been born of God and knows God.

—JOHN 4:7 (NIV)

I post a pic on Instagram.
I'm happy. I'm sad.
Snow falling atop
asphalt in one pic.
A birch tree glowing in shadow
in another.
Bernice loves it.
She clicks and she loves it.
She loves it.
She's the first,
often the only,
one to pause before each pic,
my favorite book,
a puzzling poem.
Like God, Bernice does not hesitate.
She looks and she loves it.

THE FAMILY AND I WALK OUT OF THE MALL

into the parking lot with few cars,
left like socks in a laundromat.
It's night

and my racing mind
erases me to set up tired fears
like dominoes. I forget to ask
for love back. I watch
the set up. Four decades of this.

Bernice says, *Look at the star*

THE AUNT HAS A MOMENT OF
UNDERSTANDING GOD

We stopped at a Five & Dime on the drive to the seaside.
Shach wanted gummi bears. Eshta wanted Twizzlers.
I bought them.

Back in the car, Eshta says to Shach:
I'll give you three Twizzlers for two gummi bears.

I stay silent.

God drops into our laps
dunes wrapped in
ribbons of wild grass, bows of cloud,
the sea an all-you-can-eat banquet
spread along both sides of endless shore.

Some people live
in a house on the oceanfront.
Others rent.
Others housekeep.

All of us are children
sitting in the backseat
of the car at the Five & Dime.

BERNICE ALWAYS WALKS BESIDE HER MOM. SHE WON'T WALK WITH ANYONE ELSE

"Mom, mom. We're going to the lighthouse, right?"

"Yes."

"Mom, mom."

"Yes, lighthouse," as Justa gathers flip flops, sunscreen. The keys are not in her purse.

"Mom, mom, the lighthouse, right?"

Waves surge shoreward.

THE FAMILY TAKES A TRIP TO THE LIGHTHOUSE

Earlier that morning, Justa decided to take
a beach walk.
Alone.

But the children dropped pencils and phones
at the kitchen table
to join her.

The shovel they pitched in the sand
to mark the trail through the dunes
back to the house is gone when they return.
Where are we?

They look to her.

UNCLE ESH MAKES A SURPRISE VISIT

He jumps into the hot tub,
Time for Categories! he exclaims,
finger pointing in the air.
His nieces and nephew pile in
to learn how to play
this new game under the night sky.

Animals, he decides, which means you name one
to the rhythm of claps and pats-on-the-water when it's your turn.
Two claps, then water-pat.
Cat, Esh says.
Two claps, then pat. *Skunk*, says Shach.
Two claps, a pat. *Hawk* from Eshta.
Bernice laughs *Dolphin*—then gets stumped when her turn
comes around again. She runs out of animal names, laughing
in the bubbles. Justa sits in the Adirondack chair
reading, looking up, smiling in Eden
as they clap and name God's creatures.

THE FAMILY NEVER MADE IT TO THE LIGHTHOUSE

The children ditch towels and markers
and pile into the car to visit the lighthouse.
The house quiets and the car fills
with human sound and surf.

From the backseat,
Bernice wakes from her nap
and can't find her pretzels.
"Mom, stop the car! Find my pretzels!"
Bernice unbuckles her seatbelt and throws
cups, Gatorade bottles, anything
she can find at the windshield
down the interstate
in lane-shift
construction.

"Mom! Mom! Where's my pretzels?"

A Gatorade bottle hits Justa's shoulder.
Something metal hits her elbow
then rolls between the pedals.

The plane has lost an engine
Justa is the only
one to mayday

Semis four lanes thick

"Mom! Mom!"

become meteors, objects fly

"Mom! Mom! My pretzels! Mom! Mom!"

at the dash, the door, her face
Justa kicks something that won't
move from the pedal
The other engine stalls

"Mom! Mom!"

The plane's nose pitches down
Mountain terrain rises out of nowhere

"Mom! Mom! My pretzels!"

The plane jolts
then drops like a swing

"Mom! Mom!"

Justa maneuvers the car

to the nearest exit

The mountains become smaller

They disappear from sight

Grape smell of
perspiration, soda
dripping
down her arms

She turns the car home.

Justa pulls into the driveway.
As soon as she parks,
Bernice wants to go fishing.
"Mom, mom, can I go fishing?"

Justa unlocks
the front door.

Bernice follows her inside.
"Mom, you said I could go fishing! Mom! Mom!"

Justa walks to the kitchen.
Her visage a pond.

Each mouth underneath gasping,
mutilated by a snack.

WE ALL RESURRECT

Eventually, everyone sleeps

Whether you stood on the shore,
or inched into the deepening sea,
whether waves tugged you into their hug
with claws, pinning your knees against shell
shards, or like a grandfather bounced you
on an ancient, supple knee—

After, dark sleep
And then you wake up
The sound of a glass clinking

DISABILITY SERVICES I

Bernice is home-schooled
again, expelled from her sixth school.
Administrators unfortunately do not have
resources for her
at this time.

Justa regathers documentation
for the next school placement.

Disasters she averts—the market, dog leashes,
car wrecks to the lighthouse—do not count
as evidence. Nothing to show.
No box on the form for sleepless vigilance,
for coming to see morning as an enemy,
for calming stars before they shoot.
Trauma can't be emailed as an attachment.
Post-traumatic stress disorder?
No. It's present. Lasts
as long as Justa's arms
and legs, as wide as her mind
that gets Bernice through every door,
across every interstate, up every staircase,
down hallways of locked doors,
trying every key, cutting
then sanding her own.
That steady scraping.

DISABILITY SERVICES II

Justa opens an email
from Tricia, M.A., announcing
that Bernice's IEP revision meeting
is on hold due to state policy changes for which family advocate
associates need accreditation synced with the
county office, which is implementing a new
online platform so systems are down.
Bernice's file transfers
to a temporary school caseworker
who arranges the earliest meeting next month
with the newly hired family advocate, Shapa.

In the meantime, Shapa writes, the district
will assign a tutor
to visit their home for an hour a week,
starting next month.

Erik, Support Specialist, has just sent an email from family
    services
announcing that tutoring starts three months
after the district receives geneticists' documentation
ok'ed by family advocacy services (the regional office,
not the district one).
Please send.
First, please create a new online account
with the division (the district one, not the regional)

at this link and upload documentation
from each specialist.
Justa clicks.
Error.

The scanner
in the den stopped working yesterday.
Justa will drop it off at Geek Squad on the way
to Eshta's swim meet, which starts in twenty minutes,
leaving her time to find the .pdfs she's assembled
with pediatrician documentation to forward to Tricia
(and to Shapa, to be on safe side), who won't get it
because Tricia is quitting tomorrow,
and Shapa's vacation
starts on Friday morning, so the email Justa sends
tucks itself into the abandoned inbox and goes to sleep
for two weeks.

Justa emailed William, PhD, the geneticists' documentation,
months ago, but it appears William didn't forward it to Erik.
Maybe Erik is William's replacement.

Eshta, don't forget your towel!

Click. Search.

She finds the .pdf from the pediatrician
and the neurological team. But not
from the geneticist.

Screen freezes
on the new laptop.

Did I save it
under the nurse file for school #5? #6?
In the bundle in the shoe box?

Still frozen.

Eshta! Five minutes.

Eshta has earbuds in.

WRITING WITH BERNICE

Justa shows Bernice again how to hold a pencil

    Justa cups her hand around her daughter's,
    dips the pencil into Bernice's loosening fist
    like a tulip in a jar, coaxes the girl's fingers
    into a ballet. Every three letters
    Bernice writes, she gets an M&M

    Hours ago, Justa drew Bernice a picture
    of sitting at the table to prepare her daughter
    for sitting
    Bernice screamed *Fuck you, bitch!*
    and knocked over a chair
    then raced toward the paintings framed on the kitchen wall
    but Justa got there first so Bernice could not smash them
    this time

Justa helps Bernice pick up the chair

    Justa has calmed Bernice enough
    to sit at the table and look at the letter *B*
    which Justa has written with a crayon on a scrap piece
    of paper she grabbed from the floor where the original
        worksheet
    lies in pieces like a smashed plate

Justa will worry later
about the end table Bernice hurled
at the lamp, now broken across the floor
and glittered with glass
from the television screen it shattered

Justa should've documented that
but Bernice is now

kicking through her little brother's bedroom door
after he raced there and locked it

Justa shows Bernice again how to hold a pencil

THE AUNT RECEIVES A THANK YOU CARD
IN THE MAIL

I open Bernice's card

Thnk yo Aunti
I lov the muney and card
LovBernice

I think of her sweat
and Justa's
making it up the hill of *Be*,
jumping across potholes
in *r*, hand over hand
breathless past *ni*, all lungs
and bleeding blisters through *c*,
collapsing into *e*, the finish line,
the only place in a marathon I've stood,
sipping a coffee

THE AUNT REMEMBERS
THE OUTDOOR CONCERT

We arrived at the outdoor concert early
to find a shady spot to set out

chairs and a blanket,
watermelon and brownies.

Great-grandpa wanted
to stand, stretch, and walk.
He uses a cane and moves slowly.

I'll walk with you Great-grandpa, Bernice said.

Bernice held his elbow
with her left hand and secured
his back with her right.

Great-grandpa pressed his weight
into Bernice's, who stood
secure as a boulder.

Then she synced her steps with his
inch by inch across the lawn.

THE AUNT HEARS BERNICE'S LAUGHTER

Bernice's laughter shocked me out of hunched-over
clicking and scrolling in my room

Her glee all sizes of light
filling the air with soapy-shined crystal spheres

"Isha, how did you do that? Isha, you upgraded!
Isha, dude!" she squealed into her earpiece to her partner

in the virtual video game, Isha
playing from Montana

The laughter made me look skyward,
as though Bernice were Ba'alat in the next room

I had finally arrived, late, at the Goddess's banquet
and saw the empty chair she'd been saving for me

THE TUTOR LOGS A MISSED APPOINTMENT

Bernice sits at the kitchen table
on a Monday morning in May.
Justa sits beside her,
one arm curved around her daughter's chair
like a cornerstone that holds a house
up. Justa points to the picture of the tutor,
sent by the county, who will arrive
for the first time in a few minutes.
Justa has been preparing Bernice
for the tutor's visit for weeks, pointing
to his picture every morning
and teaching Bernice to write his name.
Just now Justa places a crayon
she found on the floor into Bernice's hand
after her daughter threw the pencil.

When the tutor rings the doorbell,
coasters and vases become weapons.
Bernice shreds the picture
and lunges for Justa who tries to restrain her,
but Bernice grabs a glass filled with milk
and throws it across the room
where it shatters the framed Van Gogh
above the mantel.
Bernice runs up the stairs
where her brother Shach draws spaceships.

Diamond shards glitter the carpet
like tears from something invisible.

The tutor rings the doorbell
again. *They must not be at home.*
Irresponsible, he thinks,
logging "Missed appointment."

Checking that Shach is safe
in the locked bathroom,
Justa races downstairs to the front door,
opens it in time
to see the tutor's car
disappear down the street
like milk seeping into the couch,
into books, picture frames, the DVD player.

ODD LEAN

Reader, you too have had that moment when you knew:
I'm not like the others,
that there may be something wrong with you

I was four years old in the living room
I saw men's work boots, the most handsome shapes in the world
I slipped my foot in. I bit into that apple

Adults were in the next room
I knew I couldn't let them see me
ditch my girlhood to stand as a man
I inched behind the couch to hide my feet
I could've taken the boots off and returned to safety
but they were so manly, so me

In the carpool to soccer practice
I watch Bernice's eyes search her brother's friends'
eyes when she makes a joke
The hollow in their eyes moves away from her

Bernice knows she's been caught
wearing forbidden shoes. She tries to hide her feet

As for me, I still stand half-hidden in the living room
wearing my secret shame

Left or right, gay or straight, rich or poor,
that odd lean against the couch is one stance we all share

DAISIES IN A JAR

The school psychologist points out

                    to Justa
            who already knows

that home-schooling isn't best for Bernice
Let's gather documentation to apply to a different school
next month, he advises

At dinner, Justa reminds Bernice
to use her fork, not her fingers
Though it feels like writing with her foot,
Bernice tries

"There you go," Justa encourages

Bernice asks what's for dessert

"Ice cream," Justa says
"Ice cream?" Bernice asks. "Mom. Ice cream? Mom. Mom"
"Yes, ice cream"
"Mom! What's for dessert, Mom? Ice cream, Mom. Ice cream?
    Mom"
"Yes"

"Just checking, Mom"

"Mom. Mom"

Justa looks at daisies she's arranged in a jar
Heaven is small

BERNICE FISHING

I sit at the edge of the dock and look
across the calm lake
There's just one line to see,
my fishing wire, so soft
it fades into air

Here it's different from school
—banners shouting yellow and blue,
desks and lockers and numbers
slamming

So different from home
—jackets zipping and shoes lacing,
everyone moving
in and out of rooms
like a dock spinning

Toys, donuts, pens
Fishing lines in a tangle forever

But here it's just the blank sky,
the sleeping lake

Sometimes I catch a dream

A fish bites
and tugs me toward the stillness

I pull the fish in
The dream has given me a gift
It doesn't matter whether the fish
is big or small
All that matters is the fish wanted
what I had to give

SHACH DOESN'T WANT ANYTHING
FOR HIS BIRTHDAY

No presents please, Shach says.
No money.
No cards.
No dinner.

Shach doesn't want to bring new toys
or old friends into the house.
Change triggers Bernice's meltdowns, and Shach
doesn't want his soccer trophies broken on his birthday.

Shach doesn't want to go out to eat,
or to get a special dinner at home.
The threat of Bernice flipping over the table
outweighs the taste of double-fudge birthday cake.

If Shach gets $20, Bernice might take it
or shred it. It's best to keep money
out of the house.

I was on a walk with Shach,
and he spotted a $20 bill lying on the sidewalk.
Look, he said, like a dog noticing a phone ringing,
then yawning and returning to sleep.

BERNICE TRIUMPHS IN THE KITCHEN

My mom asked me to set the table
like I always do at 6 p.m. for dinner

Today I didn't want to. I was angry
at my brother Shach, who had gotten gummi bears
from a friend, and he shared only one with me

And then my sister Eshta had laughed
when I fell off my bike. I stuffed this hurt
away in a backpack pocket you never use

When Mom said, "Bernice, table please,"
I could feel it

The monster opened its eyes from its sleep,
began to wiggle its fingers and toes

I told it to stop wiggling, to go back to sleep

It looked at me with its sleepy eyes
and obeyed

THE CANAANITE WOMAN SEES BERNICE TRIUMPH IN THE KITCHEN

I see her
struggling to pull it together

I see her
hands leaving the plates resting on the counter

and not sending them like bullets
through the air, through the window

For every meltdown, there are two triumphs
when Bernice talks the tsunami

down. Even Poseidon
couldn't calm each storm

By the third surge she's exhausted

Think of a plastic cone
standing its ground

at the coast to hold off the sea
with its unfathomable longing

BERNICE'S AUNT HAS A DEMON

Bernice never had a demon.
I did.

My demon was that I saw her as a demon.
Whenever I decided to see Bernice
as God does—perfect, innocent—
I was healed.

Whenever my sickness came back,
whenever I raged inside at Bernice
for calling Justa lazy
because she wouldn't stop the car
on the interstate to find her pretzels,
or whenever my voice inside wanted her
to evaporate like Hiroshima
when she unplugged the vacuum cleaner
until Justa gave her money,
I asked God for the willingness
to let Him correct me.

My demon would look at me, then,
knowing that it was about to vanish
and then not knowing anything
because it was gone.
My demon instantly came back,
but more and more almost politely
asking to.

THE FAMILY LEAVES THE BEACH A DAY EARLY

The forecast: rain.
It will wipe out the one road in and out of the island.

Justa packs the shoes, the flip flop in the living room
and the one under the couch, the phone chargers on the counter
and the one fallen behind the desk; she places toothbrushes
in separate cases and gathers the milk, broccoli, and oatmeal
into the one box, gathers the sheets into the blue bag
and places it on the washing machine as the instructions
on the refrigerator from the beach house rental company
say to. Everything goes into the Thule
which she unlatches, fills, and retightens with one arm
while her other arm secures bags between car seats.

We're driving back to the mainland. I sit in the passenger seat
in a dream of feeling, gazing across the sea.

The clouds, she says.
Look at them gathering.

Grey, thick. We're leaving just in time.

THE CANAANITE WOMAN SEES A RAINBOW

Driving back home from the sea,
six more hours to go,
Justa looked into the sky
A rainbow!

I saw a sliver of it,
then noticed another rainbow on the other side of the sky

Two rainbows, I said

It's one rainbow, she corrected me,

Look how the pieces fade
and then unite when you follow them up

THE CANAANITE YOUNG WOMAN
GOES TO COLLEGE

At home, her cereal bowl lays quiet
in the cupboard. The hair dryer falls
into a deep sleep. Our dog is restless,
doesn't have her warm body to doze against.
The stereo won't speak.
Michael Jackson won't sing.

I find a journal in a box,
filled with quotations she had copied down
from Erica Jong, Albert Einstein, Toni Morrison.
Her handwriting is careful to trace
beauty and truth, as if she thought they
weren't hers yet. As if they're a tightrope
she inches across, the pen her balancing pole.
But there's a flourish in the careful letters,
as though she wants to fall off their lines.

THE CANAANITE WOMAN'S SEVENTH BOOK

The stove warms
with grains and carrots colorful as rainforest.
Chicken and pasta with rosemary sprinkles.
Garlic beef with avocado and tomatoes.
Basil leaves from the garden.

"Protein, whole grains, and a half plate of vegetables
for every meal," Bernice says, showing me her plate.

Justa lights a candle.
The flame gleams across forks on the left,
spoons on the right. Darkness
is soft light.

Justa curates a home.
This is her gallery.
Her own paintings hang on the wall behind the table
alongside Van Gogh's.
She's almost done writing her seventh book.
Alice Munro, Emily Dickinson,
and Rumi scooch over to make room on the shelf.
They live here. They sit by her.

MOM, MOM

A call Bernice doesn't think to silence
when it may no longer be considered age-appropriate
to call out for your mother.

She calls *Mom* enough times to make up for the times
others lock *Mom* under their tongues,
for all who wanted to call for their mother
but didn't, or who call for their mother
and she never came, or never anymore.

Gilgamesh to Ninsun,
Achilles to Thetis, Persephone
to Demeter, Yeshua to Maryam,
street vendors calling in the cup of coffee
they pass to you, you calling in your hand reaching
for the warmth, in the doctor's pause after your question,
the quiet throne holding the queen.

When everyone else has left

the party,
returned to the mainland,
fled the waiting room,
left the cross,

who remains

but mom.
Mom.

Bernice lets Justa know
she sees her.

MATTHEW AND MARK ONLY GOT PART OF IT

Jesus called *Mom, Mom, why has God forsaken me?*
We don't know what her response was.
We just know she was there.

THE AUNT'S ARRIVAL

Morning.
It was time
for me to leave.

Bags packed, car loaded,
I walked to Shach
who reclined on the living room
couch, nesting in the branches of his inner oak.
He dutifully stood up, climbed down
for the farewell hug
then returned to the couch
to ascend his branches.

Eshta came out
with her rabbit to say goodbye.
She held its delicate, quick body for me
to pet its silky-grey head.
Her hands protected
its soft liveliness squeezed between
Eshta's and mine for the final hug.

I walked upstairs
to Bernice's room,
knocked on her door.

Bernice?

Come in,

I could just make out from the other side,
yet heard something full,
ready
in the sound,
like wings awake, vigorous, working
even when folded.

She had been napping,
but sat up as I rounded the bed.
She held her arms out
toward me
in the half darkness
as if she knew
I, too, must one day
open my eyes
and stretch my wings
to fellow butterflies
in our common darkness,

suddenly soft, cool, and quiet,
furnished with lamps.

A stylish desk and chairs.
A couch with pillows.
Beanbags. A shag rug.
A consul with several video game controls.
Three yoga mats.

Potted plants
with wide green leaves.

A priestess

had been here,
before Bernice, before me,
had studied darkness's dimensions
and surveyed its walls,
had said *This will never do*
—so installed rice-paper light fixtures,
ordered plush comforters, hauled in
recliners, a queen-sized bed, a lavender
scent diffuser glowing on a small table.
A hint of tea tree and mint.
The gentle sound of a fan.

Fresh clothes folded in a laundry
basket. A shirt, pants, underwear
and socks placed neatly on a chair.
Shoes arranged by the door.

THE CANAANITE WOMAN
CATCHES HER BREATH

Justa brings Bernice through entrances:
children's museums, skating rinks, libraries, beaches,
musicals, parks, hospitals whose mystified doctors

try their best, but the appointment is over before it began.
Bernice loses it in the waiting room

and hurls magazines
at the receptionist before grabbing an end table
and flinging it at the glass. Justa's brother Esh
uses Judo to restrain Bernice until hospital police arrive.
A nurse gives Bernice a tranquilizer.

Justa squeezed in a run three mornings in a row
by returning the call to the special education lawyer
in the afternoon after consoling her son Shach
when Bernice destroyed his baseball cards,
and after comforting Eshta when Bernice
smashed her doll castle, and after assuring
Bernice that her pet turtle was unhurt
after Eshta stole it in retaliation and threatened
to throw it into the creek, to which Bernice responded
by upturning Eshta's vanity. At least it wasn't the fish aquarium
this time. They swim in soft light.

Justa does weight training on Tuesday.
She was booking her annual trip to Denver
with college friends when Bernice hurled her medication
against the window. The dog ran to eat the pills.
Eventually Justa got Bernice to take them.
She can't remember how. She's over it.
Shach needs picked up from swim practice,
and Justa can't arrive in time (the medication-flinging),
so she calls a neighbor, asks if he can drive Shach home
while she races after Bernice whose "Shut up!"
came from across the street.

Justa sees red wine pooling on tiles.

Denver waits on the screen, then goes blank.

By 5 p.m. Justa climbs the bleachers
as Bernice steps onto the softball field
to gather equipment
wearing her pressed uniform.

"Hey, how are ya?" another mom waves Justa down.
The question takes her breath away.

Justa's grace like God's.
No one cheers the catch.

THE LIVING ROOM IS DARK, EMPTY, AND QUIET

Denver flicks back onto the screen.
On the table, the flowers,
heads bent in darkness,
notice grains in the wood.

Sepia. Chestnut.
Splashes of gold.
A color not quite umber.

THE HOSPITAL POLICEMEN

At school-placement #7, maybe 9,
teachers avert their eyes as Justa enters,
still in yoga gear.
She got the phone call while rolling out her mat
that the police are at school again to restrain her daughter.
She rerolled her mat.

Heading to the school doors, Justa counts them:
six policemen surround Bernice, in handcuffs.
One officer shouts obscenities at Bernice,
who shouts back.

But in the hospital waiting room, a week later,
the policemen calm her. Bernice has
knocked over tables, thrown chairs.
Magazines play dead, strewn across the floor.
The room empty of patients who fled.
Bernice's doctor appointment,
over before it began.

An officer has Bernice pinned to the floor
softly, his knee arranged upon her back
like a blanket. Bernice relaxes,
her cheek rests like a pillow
against industrial carpet as they await

the physician's order
for a tranquilizer.

You're safe now, honey, one policeman says to Bernice.
Don't worry, Ma'am. We do this all the time, another officer as-
    sures Justa.
It's ok. It's ok,
they repeat like a mantra.
Justa's body decides if it can trust corpse pose.

THE CANAANITE WOMAN
DOES MOUNTAIN POSE

Mountains shake,
finding their balance

Their sweat rolls
as stones across the parking
lot, somehow absorbed
between couch cushions

The nature of mountain
is to drip into more
angles of light

QUEEN MOTHER

A friend asked if I was close to my sister.
One is close to queens the way Beyoncé's fans are close to
    Beyoncé.
You behold. You applaud and bow down.

BERNICE VISITS HER GRANDPARENTS

Mom's not telling me five more minutes for video games.
I don't have to look at the knives and remember.
My brother's friends aren't here. No side eyeing
when I share a joke.

Here at my grandparents' house, I walk into summer snowfall.
The world is new for two weeks. Light refracting light.

Grandpa takes me fishing and laughs
when he reminds me of our game: I can ask him three questions.
I get a sticker for each question, but I give him a sticker
when I goof and ask a fourth. I've lost only once.

Grandma takes me to the corner market
to buy chocolate chips for pancakes. I'm allowed inside.

No video games, and it could be boring,
but the space for quiet moving in and out doors,
up and down stairs, to and from stores makes my mind
feel like snow patting meadow
all the way to the frozen pond where no one fishes
except Grandpa and me. When I get home, a tower of pancakes
I don't worry to share. Winter warmth
in the summer.

RAINBOW TALK TIME

At bedtime Justa sits on Eshta's bed
and clicks on the rainbow prism lamp.
Streaks of color bathe the room
in pinks, yellows, and oranges.
Star stickers glow across the ceiling.
Rainfall of light sprinkles the comforter.
Eshta, an astronaut floating under covers,
shares valleys, plateaus, and mountains
of her day filled with swimming and friends,
imaginary hotels for dolphins. In the dark,
under a galaxy of stars, in a heaven of pastels,
Justa shows Eshta how to breathe
in outer space, how to make
a black hole luminous.

SHACH'S RAINBOW TALK TIME

I go inside Shach's room with my sister to hug him good night.
His mom sits beside him on the bed,
leans over to tuck him in.
Good nights all around.

She and I leave.
But he calls her back.

She goes inside.
He wants just her.
With the door closed.

So God, too, rises
from His warm chair
in the room's cool darkness,
steps quietly into the hall,
closing the door softly
to mother, son, and their Holy Ghost,
not His.

BERNICE GOES TO BED

She comes downstairs after video games
to where her mother writes.
It's their shared ritual.
Mom, come up and say goodnight, Mom.
Bernice is the last child to sleep.
Yes, I will in a minute, Justa assures her every night.
Bernice turns and walks back upstairs
to her bedroom, her steps
light as a stone skipping
across the lace of lake.
Justa has made her a college dormroom
up there, straight out of *Better Homes and Gardens,*
a broad mat under the bed, organizers on her desk,
posters framed on the wall, bamboo and ferns,
her own couch. Bernice's room how she wants it
—Justa's presence tucked into every folder,
rounding every pillow, steeled as prongs
powering the nightlights beside her bed,
by the door, down the hallway, along the stairs,
every up and down.

THE CANAANITE WOMAN LOOKS OUT
THE KITCHEN WINDOW AT NIGHT.
SHE SEES HERSELF ILLUMINATING

What will you do
when darkness comes?
Every twelve hours
you get the chance to practice.
Will you seek solitude
or ache for another's arms?
Will you freeze in fear
or this time fly? Will you drink
or is the craving gone?
Grab a sweater or pull one off?
Walk or become still?
Snack or fast?
Go to bed or stay up?
Clean or leave the dishes?
There is a finite amount of things
to do when darkness comes.
Notice, next time, what you do.
Are you surprised
or nodding because you knew?

THE CANAANITE WOMAN
SITS ATOP THE BOULDER

After good nights, Justa hangs on to the edge of sleep.
She doesn't want to see dawn as another enemy.
Stars inside her show her how to get to morning.

On hikes through woods,
Eshta brings Justa twigs with magical swirls,
rocks with tunnels of ruby, bugs she coaxes from branches.
"Mom." *Crunch.* "Mom" *Crunch.*
Shach makes a four-leaf clover and brings it to her.

Through snow, over mud.
Through leaves. Across puddles.
In rain they carry umbrellas.
In sun they wear sunscreen.
They wear boots. Flip flops.
Cleats. Crocs.
They walk past blooming trees.
They walk past barren trees
harboring blooms.
"Mom. Mom!"

We pause near a boulder. Justa sits on it.
I snap a photograph.
Peace lasts the duration of a shutter click.

Darkness closes in to create a field of light.
Opening after closing whenever the button is pressed.

Some call Jesus a savior. I call him a survivor.
To resurrect is to turn the other cheek
for the bite of changing perspective again.
Is Easter trauma or miracle?
Rise and walk into the unkempt garden.
Let others be shocked.

Justa sits atop the boulder.

She's already left it.

She's leagues ahead of figs then fishing
and meadows more verdant than magical clover.
Her eyes discern seas of rainbow Noah never imagined.
With greater grace than butterflies, Justa swims
waves of too much light until she's above them,
walking on water I do not dare dip my toe in.
Rocks with crystals fall where they will.

We follow her.

JESUS'S CHIEF OF STAFF EMAILS THE
CANAANITE WOMAN

Dear Ms. Justa,

Jesus of Nazareth has asked that I write to you. As you know, you made an extraordinary impression on him during his visit to the region of Tyre. It is not every day that Jesus is dumbstruck by such fierce persistence and athletic love as he witnessed in you. You opened Jesus's eyes to a new dimension of God.

You had shared with us at that time that due to other duties, you were unable to accept our offer to join our team. However, we wonder if your circumstances have changed and if you might reconsider our offer. We write to ask again if you might consider joining our ministry, this time as its official photographer and writer.

We have been following your work, and we find your photographs and accompanying stories breathtaking. Your photography and writing bring out lights and darks of the seemingly mundane—bleachers at the soccer game, biking down the sidewalk—and reveal the sacred in everything and everyone, in all its darkness and light, in all the nuanced shades between.

Our work opens new, often startling dimensions to the sacred as well. As our ministry expands across the Mediterranean, we seek to grow our staff. Your work would entail traveling with us and documenting Jesus's talks and healings in temples, public gardens, and private homes. Won't you please consider embarking on this journey with us?

We sadly admit that the pay is modest, though your expenses would be minimal. We are housed and fed by those who host us at temples and homes. Yet we hope the chance to travel and spread your art across the region to support our mission of extending God's love might tempt you to reconsider our offer. We are gaining esteem with an interfaith community of rabbis, artists, and philosophers across Judea and the Mediterranean into Egypt and Greece. Joining us might open doors for you professionally, artistically, and personally while also spreading God's love.

We would be delighted to continue this conversation in more detail over lunch or dinner at a time convenient for you. Please get in touch with us at the email address or phone number provided, and I will be happy to arrange a meal for you to share with Jesus of Nazareth directly. He would love the opportunity to tell you more about this position and to answer any questions you might have.

Jesus looks forward to your response.

God's Peace be with You,
Peter of Galilee

THE CANAANITE WOMAN READS THE EMAIL

I haven't answered yet
I'm savoring the glow
—my work seen as work,
found beautiful, and sought

Join Jesus's team and travel across the Mediterranean
Wow. Akhenaten's abandoned city. Plato's Parthenon
Ishtar's Temple in Damascus. Maybe in a few years
when Bernice is an adult. Though she'll be living with me

A friend told me she wanted to write novels
but wrote short stories instead because she's a mother
She holds too many characters living countless storylines
to fit into one book

I wonder how unified Jesus's ministry would be
if he were a mother. Would he believe in one God
or several. One love or many. One ending or all of them

Maybe that's why he wants me on his team
I know a trinity he doesn't

Mother, Daughter, and Holy Ghost

NOTES

"Nevertheless, She Persisted": This phrase from the introduction comes from US Senator Mitch McConnell, who in 2017 used this term to chastise fellow Senator Elizabeth Warren's refusal to stop her argument against the confirmation of Jeff Sessions to the position of US Attorney General. Though McConnell's phrase was meant to rebuke Warren's speech, it instead became a feminist rallying cry, celebrating women's persistence to express their points of view in the face of systemic pressures to obey patriarchal authority without question.

"The Canaanite Woman and Her Daughter Refine Jesus's Taste" and "The Aunt Hears Bernice's Laughter": Ba'alat is a primary goddess and wife of the god Ba'al in some ancient forms of Canaanite religion.

"The Canaanite Woman and Her Daughter Refine Jesus's Taste"; "Clement, the Dog"; "Bernice Walks Clement": I named the family dog "Clement"—who possesses mystical qualities—before I learned that "Clement" is also the supposed name of an early writer who names both the Canaanite woman (Justa) and her daughter (Bernice) in the text known as *The Clementine Homilies* (200–300 AD). Perhaps the writer Clement was calling to me from another realm to include him overtly in the book.

"The Canaanite Woman Reads the Email": The lines "A friend told me she wanted to write novels / but wrote short stories instead because she's a mother" owe a debt to a CBC (*Canadian Broadcasting Company*) article entitled "90 Things to Know about Master Short Story Writer Alice Munro" (April 2017), which states that

87

Munro "turned to short stories when she started writing because, as a housewife with three young daughters, she didn't have the time to devote to a novel" (para. 4).

CPSIA information can be obtained
at www.ICGtesting.com
Printed in the USA
BVHW032213310722
643334BV00009B/16